Do|Breakfast!

Tasty Treats to Kick Start your Day

Do Breakfast!

Tasty Treats to Kick Start your Day

Edited by Jane Donovan

SILVERBACK

A QUINTET BOOK

This edition published by Silverback Books, Inc.
San Francisco

ISBN 1-930603-23-1

This book was designed and produced by
Quintet Publishing Limited
6 Blundell Street
London N7 9BH

Creative Director: Richard Dewing
Designer: Paul Elmes
Project Editor: Debbie Foy
Editor: Jane Donovan

Typeset in Great Britain by Central Southern
Typesetters, Eastbourne
Manufactured in China by Regent Publishing
Services Limited
Printed in China by SNP Leefung
Printers Limited

Contents

Introduction

Rise and shine to this indulgent collection of recipes that have been specially designed to ensure the perfect start to your day. The ideas have been created for special occasions, relaxed weekends, or when there is enough time to enjoy your own company. In this selection of delicious recipes there are suggestions for healthy kickstarts to the day, including cereals, shakes, and fresh fruits, traditional ideas using eggs, such as Eggs Benedict and Omelet Fines Herbes, and a whole collection of breakfast bakes that are surprisingly easy to make.

In addition to the recipes, the basics of great breakfasts are also covered, with advice on how to make a classic cappuccino, hot tips for perfect eggs, juicing, and recipes for spreads and preserves that are traditionally served at breakfast time. So wake up to the delicious aroma of freshly brewed coffee and stimulate your senses with wafts of warmed bread. This book is a visual feast of ideas – breakfast will never be the same again!

Ingredients

Often the most successful recipes rely on just a few carefully chosen ingredients. Here are some ideas for breakfast ingredients that you will want to keep in your refrigerator or store cupboard.

Espresso and Specialty Coffees should be purchased regularly in small amounts so that none of the flavor is lost. Buy directly from the roaster where possible for the freshest coffee. Store coffee, either as beans or ground, in a cool place. If your home is very warm, you may like to keep coffee in the refrigerator but keep it well wrapped to avoid moisture getting through. Always store coffee in a dark place and remember that it is only at its best for 10 days to two weeks as beans, and ground coffee starts to lose its flavor after just a couple of days. If you buy in bulk, coffee can be stored, well wrapped, in the freezer. Even so, it will only be in peak condition for about four weeks.

Instant Coffee For the best flavor, most freeze-dried blends have been developed to be made with one teaspoon of coffee in a six fluid-ounce cup. As with beans, you get what you pay for and the more expensive brands are definitely worth the extra cost. Instant coffee loses its flavor in the same way as freshly ground and coffee beans, so buy in small jars of good-quality freeze-dried instant coffee and use it quickly.

Specialty Teas Good retailers store loose leaf teas in large airtight caddies and sell them by weight according to your requirements. Buy in small quantities at first to make sure that the tea is to your taste. Even then, as tea dries out quickly, store small amounts at home to avoid spoiling the flavor. Always ask to see tea before you buy. The dry leaves should have an even, pleasant appearance with particles of roughly the same size. When brewed, the infusion should be clear. Black teas should give a bright, reddish infusion; oolongs are generally orangy-brown to dark brown brews, and the liquor from green teas should be pale yellowish-green.

Organic Fruits and Vegetables will produce the most natural and uncontaminated juiced drinks and light breakfast meals. They tend to be more expensive, and there is less of a range than standard varieties, but they have not been exposed to chemical treatments or waxes. Remember that many essential nutrients are contained in thinner skinned produce, so avoid peeling where possible.

Start by drinking small amounts of juice each day, up to 10 fluid ounces to begin with, and gradually build up the amount you consume. This will ensure that your body gets used to a more concentrated form of nutrition. Always dilute dark green and dark red vegetable juices by four parts to one, remembering that they are potent cleansers. If you suffer from sugar intolerance, diabetes, or candidiasis, you should be wary of the amount of fruit juice you drink.

Honey has been used as a food medicine for thousands of years. The nutritional content varies, but all honey consists of about 25 per cent water; the rest is glucose and a little fructose. Although honey is better for you than refined sugar, it is still an energy provider and not much else, so it should only be used in restricted amounts. However, it also has antiseptic properties, is easy to swallow, and is soothing and calming.

Seeds can be eaten on their own or combined with yogurts, drinks, or cereals. Buy in small quantities and store airtight containers in a cool place. Try pumpkin seeds, sesame, and sunflower from health stores and supermarkets.

Yogurt is made from milk and is one of the finest natural foods available. It can be made from whole or skim milk, left natural or flavored—always check the labels for added ingredients, such as artificial colors, flavorings, and sugars. Greek yogurt is a

variety that has been strained, and is more concentrated and creamy.

Yogurt is a good source of protein, and low-fat varieties are especially recommended. It is high in calcium and other minerals like potassium, magnesium, and the B-vitamin complex.

Eggs are always a useful stand-by and lend themselves to so many recipes. They provide nutrients, proteins, fats, vitamins, and minerals. Eggs purchased from a supermarket with a quick turnover can be stored in a cool place for up to two weeks. Avoid the refrigerator as most recipes call for eggs at room temperature. For the best flavor of all, try fresh free-range farm eggs.

Eggs can also be added to drinks for extra protein and substance but should be omitted if the drinks are to be made for the elderly, young babies, pregnant women, or people with immune-deficient systems as they may contain salmonella. Cooking eggs eliminates the risk of salmonella poisoning, but as some drinks use raw or lightly cooked eggs, take heed of the above considerations during preparation.

Herbs and Spices are the perfect way to "pep up" healthy drinks and other recipes. Not only do they add flavor and aroma, but they also have their own special properties and nutrients. For the freshest of flavors, you could even grow your own herbs in a window box outside the kitchen.

Flour is the main ingredient in breads and the gluten contained in flour gives bread and baked goods their structure. All-purpose and whole wheat flours can be used separately or combined for different textures. Other flours

and grains, such as corn, oat, rye, cornmeal, oatmeal, wheat grain, bran, and rice, can add variety and texture. Most of the baked recipes in this book call for all-purpose flour.

Fats such as butter, margarine, oil, lard, and suet add flavor, moistness, and color to breads. Light-textured oils, such as sunflower or canola, are best for muffins and quick breads. Avoid blended oils as they are not so reliable. You may prefer salted butter to use as a spread, but generally the unsalted variety is best for baking as it usually has a lower moisture content, and the amount of salt in the recipe can be more easily controlled. Unless a recipe stipulates chilled or cold butter, always soften butter to room temperature before use.

Leaveners Many of the baked recipes in this book use chemical raising agents, such as baking powders and sodas, to raise a batter. Most modern baking powders contain two raising agents; one begins to work as soon as the liquid is added, and the other is heat-activated. For this reason, mixtures containing baking powder must be mixed quickly, and then baked immediately. Baking soda is often used in combination with other acid ingredients, such as buttermilk, molasses, or sour cream. Raising agents, such as baking powders and sodas, should be stored in a cool, dark place, and replaced every three to four months to ensure freshness.

Sweeteners, ranging from sugar to honey, or maple syrup or molasses, add flavor and moisture to different breads. They bring out flavors and are often added to savory muffins, scones, or quick breads. Sweeteners also improve the keeping quality of baked goods.

Yeast is the raising agent used to make most breads, and is also in many sweet-yeast doughs used for coffeecakes and sweet-yeast breads. It is available in three forms: fresh or compressed, active-dry yeast, and easy-blend. The recipes in this book use active-dry yeast since it is more easily available.

Equipment

Most of the recipes in this book can be recreated using the basic kitchen utensils found in every home. However, if you like muffins, it is worth investing in new, nonstick bakeware as minimal greasing is required. For this, use a vegetable greasing spray. Paper and foil liners are additions for baking, as are loaf pans (9 x 5 x 3-inch or 8 x 4 x 2½-inch) and flour dredgers. Cushion-air baking sheets are excellent for breads and coffeecakes to prevent the underside burning before the bread is baked through.

Every cook should have two skillets, one with an 8-inch diameter base and another a 10-inch. Heavy, cast-iron pans are best and when new, it is always best to follow the manufacturer's instructions on seasoning your cookware.

For whisking and mixing, a balloon whisk is particularly useful for eggs, and so are kitchen forks (wooden ones are gentler than the metal variety). Metal teaspoons and tablespoons are essential items for every cook, but wooden spoons in different sizes and a long-handled draining spoon are also useful. Spatulas, kitchen tongs, a good set of knives, kitchen scissors, graters, and zesters will make life easier.

Finally, a food processor doing the work of both a liquidizer and a mincer; it's also excellent for shredding and slicing in large quantities, and saves you a lot of time.

Breakfast Basics

To enjoy the best breakfasts, *many of the same basic principles apply.* **Here are a few guidelines to get you started.**

Rules for Coffee Making

● Many people like a strong coffee to start the day. For a regular coffee, choose a French or Continental blend which are very darkly roasted. And for a single variety, try Java, which is rich and full in flavor, or Costa Rica coffee, which is full and mellow, but has a great depth of flavor.

● Coffee should be served as hot as possible, so do warm the pot or cups, especially when serving espresso or an espresso-based drink.

● With the exception of Arabic coffee, no coffee is made with boiling water as it scorches easily, producing a bitter flavor. Either boil a kettle and let it stand for 30 to 60 seconds before pouring, or try to catch it just as it comes to a boil. Electric coffee makers will heat the water to the optimum temperature for you.

● Purists will suggest using filtered or bottled water if the water from your faucet is heavily chlorinated or very chalky.

● Coffee should not be reheated. Although it is still drinkable, the flavor changes dramatically. It will keep hot in better condition if poured into a warmed vacuum flask, rather than keeping it on a hot plate. However, it should not be left standing for more than 30 minutes.

● The best-flavored coffee is obtained if you grind your own pre-roasted coffee beans at home just before making the coffee using a manual or electric grinder.

Tea and Food Pairings

Tea is a gourmet beverage that pairs successfully with all types of food. Just as wines are selected to enhance the flavor of certain foods, so teas may also be matched to particular savory or sweet items on the menu. Here is a guide to help you choose the right tea to pair with particular recipes or individual foods.

Types of Food	Suitable Teas
Continental-style breakfast (breads, cheese, jams, etc.)	Yunnan, Ceylon, Indonesian, Assam, Dooars, Terai, Travancore, Nilgiri, Kenya, Darjeeling
English-style breakfast (fried foods, eggs, smoked fish, ham, bacon, etc.)	Ceylon, Kenya, African blends, Assam, Tarry Souchong, Lapsang Souchong
Light savory breakfasts	Yunnan, Lapsang Souchong, Ceylon, Darjeeling, Assam, Green teas, Oolongs
Spicy foods	Keemun, Ceylon, Oolongs, Darjeeling, Green teas, Jasmine, Lapsang Souchong
Cheeses	Lapsang Souchong, Earl Grey, Green teas
Fish	Oolongs, Smoked Teas, Earl Grey, Darjeeling, Green teas
Meat	Earl Grey, Lapsang Souchong, Kenya, Jasmine

Hot Tips for Perfect Eggs

• For best results with **boiled eggs,** the eggs should be used at room temperature. If your eggs constantly crack, pierce the rounded end with a needle to release the pressure. The water for boiling should be barely simmering and the saucepan should be small enough to prevent the eggs from moving about too much during cooking. Lower the eggs carefully (using a large spoon) into gently simmering water. Simmer for exactly one minute, remove from the heat, put the lid on, and leave the eggs for a further five minutes for small eggs and five to six minutes for larger sizes.

For really fresh eggs that are less than four days old, allow extra cooking time. Serve in eggcups with hot buttered toast.

• Use really fresh eggs for **poaching.** Fill a small skillet with water to a depth of about 1½ inches and heat the water until barely simmering. Break each egg gently into the water and don't attempt to poach more than two at a time, unless you are a very experienced cook. Three minutes is just right for larger eggs, but you can vary this fractionally according to taste. Baste the tops with water while cooking. Remove with a slotted spoon and place onto paper towels to absorb excess water.

• The best way to **scramble** eggs is to melt a walnut-size piece of butter in a small solid pan over a gentle heat. Swirl it around to coat the pan thoroughly. Have two large eggs beaten and seasoned ready to add to the foaming butter. Stir quickly using a wooden spoon and get the point right into the corners of the pan to avoid the eggs sticking. Remove the pan from the heat, and add an extra touch of butter to melt into the eggs as they finish cooking.

For extra indulgence, you could add a teaspoonful of heavy cream along with the second piece of butter. For a more healthy option, try snipped pieces of smoked salmon or fresh chives.

• **Baked eggs or Eggs en Cocotte** (see page 33) can be cooked with a whole range of other ingredients such as cheese, cream, and lightly cooked vegetables. For perfect results every time, use ramekin dishes that have been generously buttered.

• Use an enameled cast-iron or heavy aluminum skillet for **omelet making.** A two-egg omelet requires a six-inch pan, while a heartier four- or five-egg omelet calls for a 10-inch pan. Break the eggs into a basin and avoid over-beating them. A large fork or blade of a knife is all you need for this. Season with salt and fresh black pepper.

Heat the pan over medium heat to warm through. When hot, throw in a good knob of butter, turn the heat up to its highest, and swirl the butter around to coat the sides and pan base thoroughly. When the butter begins to bubble, pour in the eggs (shake the pan to spread them out evenly), then take a fork or spoon and draw the edges of the omelet toward the center of the pan, allowing liquid pools of egg to run into the spaces you have made. Continue until the omelet is almost set but the surface is soft and a little liquid. Tilt the pan onto the edge of a warm plate, then flip the omelet edge over to the center using a fork or spoon. Fold it over again as you turn it out of the pan.

For a more buttery flavor, add a little melted butter to the eggs before you pour them into the pan. The best omelets are often the simplest and if you add fillings, use just a little as the eggs are the most important part of this dish (see Omelet Fines Herbes, page 35).

● Use a heavy skillet for **fried eggs.** Heat the butter or oil slowly and then remove the skillet from the heat to break in the eggs. (If you prefer, break the eggs separately into a cup first.) Return to the heat and cook slowly until the white is a solid color. While cooking, you can baste the egg yolk with the hot fat to pinken it. Alternatively, once the white is cooked, remove the pan from the heat and flip the egg with a spatula or serve sunny-side up.

● **Eggy bread** is a delicious breakfast snack and goes particularly well with crispy bacon. Whisk two or three eggs in a bowl and season well. Add a little milk. Dip a slice of bread into the egg mixture and leave until thoroughly soaked. Meanwhile, heat oil or butter in a skillet until hot, then add the eggy bread. Cook until the bread appears omelet-like, then turn over and cook the other side. Serve immediately.

Handy Hints for Breakfast Bakes

● Avoid overmixing batters. Stir wet and dry ingredients together until just combined; the batter should be slightly lumpy.

● Have your ingredients ready and at room temperature before you begin, especially butter and eggs.

● Bake cakes and breads in a single layer on the middle oven-shelf or rack as soon as they are mixed, since both baking powder and soda begin their raising action as soon as they are moistened.

● For an evenly-rounded muffin top, grease only the bottom and half an inch up the side of the cup. To avoid soggy muffins, remove from the pan almost immediately after removing from the oven. Cool quick breads for slightly longer.

● Check for doneness after the minimum baking time indicated.

● Day-old muffins, scones, and biscuits can be split and toasted, then served with butter or preserves for a delicious breakfast treat.

● Never over-knead biscuit or scone dough.

● For soft-sided cookies, bake them closely together. Arrange shapes at least two inches apart for a crispier finish.

● Use a thermometer to check liquids before adding yeast and choose a warm place for raising dough.

● Knead dough by folding it, then push down and away from you with the heel of your hand, slightly curving your fingers over the edge. Turn the dough and repeat.

● For raising dough, place in an oiled bowl, turning to coat thoroughly with oil to prevent a crust forming over the surface. Alternatively, slide the dough in its bowl into a large, plastic bag, and seal tightly, allowing room for expansion.

● To check if dough has doubled in volume, press your finger into it. If the hole remains, the dough is ready to be punched down.

● To punch down dough, push your fist into the center of the dough, pulling the edges to the center, then knead once or twice. Alternatively, turn the dough onto a lightly floured surface; it will automatically deflate. Knead once or twice.

Preserves, Butters, and Spreads

A good selection of sweet and savory preserves and spreads is essential for any breakfast table. As with tea and coffee, *buy the best you can afford* from good-quality food stores and delicatessens, and try these simple, *but delicious recipes.*

Tropical Fruit Preserve

makes about 4 lb

2 lb cooking apples, peeled and sliced
Juice and shells of 4 limes
2 mangoes, peeled and chopped
5 cups water
6 cups sugar
6 passionfruit, strained

Place the apples in a large pan. Tie all the peel in a piece of cheesecloth with the lime shells and mango trimmings. Place in the pan. Add the lime juice and water. Simmer for 1 hour.

Remove the bag of trimmings. Add the sugar, mango, and passionfruit to the pan. Heat gently, stirring until the sugar dissolves. Bring to a boil and cook until setting point. Pour into freshly sterilized pots, cover, and label.

Strawberry and Gooseberry Preserve

makes about 5 lb

1½ lb gooseberries
⅔ cup water
1½ lb strawberries, hulled
6 cups sugar

Wash and trim the gooseberries and place in a preserving pan with the water. Cook gently until softened. Add the strawberries and continue cooking until the fruit is soft. Remove the pan from the heat and stir in the sugar until dissolved.

Return the pan to the heat. Bring to a boil, stirring to make sure the sugar has completely dissolved. Cook rapidly until setting point is reached. Leave to stand for 5 minutes. Pour into warmed, sterilized jars, cover, label, and date.

Seville Orange Marmalade

makes about 7 lb

3 lb Seville oranges
12½ cups water
10 cups sugar
Juice of 2 lemons

Scrub the oranges and place in a large pan with the water. Bring to a boil, cover, and reduce the heat. Simmer for 2 to 2¼ hours until the oranges are soft. Remove the fruit with a slotted spoon, reserving the liquid in the pan. Leave to cool.

Cut the oranges in half, remove the pits, and slice the flesh as thinly as possible. Return the oranges to the pan. Add the sugar and lemon juice and heat gently, stirring, until the sugar is completely dissolved.

Bring to a boil and boil hard until setting point is reached. Remove any scum and leave to stand for 15 minutes before pouring into warmed, sterilized jars. Cover, label, and date.

Maple-Walnut Butter

makes about ¾ cup

1 stick butter, softened
1 Tbsp maple syrup
⅓ cup toasted walnuts, chopped fine

In a medium bowl with an electric mixer, beat the softened butter until light and creamy. Beat in the maple syrup, then stir in the walnuts until blended. Spoon into a bowl and refrigerate, covered, until ready to serve, then soften at room temperature.

Mint Butter

makes about ¾ cup

1 stick butter
¼ cup extra-virgin olive oil
12 large mint leaves

Put the butter, oil, and mint leaves in the bowl of a food processor fitted with the metal blade. Process 30 to 60 seconds until well blended, scraping down the side of the bowl once or twice. Store, covered, in the refrigerator. Soften at room temperature before serving.

Orange Butter

makes about ¾ cup

1 stick butter, (unsalted or salted), softened
2 to 3 Tbsp sugar (or to taste)
3 tsp grated orange rind
1 Tbsp orange juice

Beat the butter, sugar, and orange rind until soft, creamy, and well blended. Add the orange juice gradually to combine. Refrigerate, covered, until ready to serve. Soften at room temperature before serving.

Green Onion Cream-Cheese Spread

makes about 1 cup

6 oz cream cheese, softened
4 Tbsp freshly chopped herbs, such as parsley, dillweed, chives, and basil
1 to 2 green onions, chopped fine
Salt and freshly ground black pepper

In a medium bowl, beat the cream cheese with the herbs and onions until well blended. Season to taste and store, covered, in the refrigerator until ready to serve.

Ginger Cream-Cheese Spread

makes about 1 cup

8 oz cream cheese, softened
2 Tbsp firmly packed brown sugar, or honey
¼ cup ginger marmalade

Beat the cream cheese together with the sugar or honey until soft and creamy and well blended. Add in the marmalade. Store, covered, in the refrigerator until ready to serve.

Hot Drinks,
Juices,
and
Shakes

Perfect Espresso

If you are serious about coffee, *then you need an espresso machine.* **For best results, use fine-ground coffee and keep practicing!** *Making espresso is a passion* **and takes time to perfect the art. A standard espresso is about 1½ fluid ounces and** *served in tiny coffee cups;* **it is little more than a mouthful so** *many people order a double.*

Commercially ground fine coffee (allow 1½ to 2 Tbsp per cup)
Water, as required
Sugar, to taste

TIP Crema is the mark of a good espresso. It is caused by the essential volatile oils from the coffee mixing with water and air as coffee is made. A good crema is evenly colored and covers the whole surface of the coffee in the cup.

1 Fill the espresso machine with water according to the manufacturer's instructions. Wait for the water to heat and use this time to heat the espresso cups. These can also be run under hot water from a faucet and left for a few minutes before drying.

2 Pack the coffee down tightly into the filter basket using a tamper. This is very much trial and error: if coffee is packed too tightly, the water will drip through slowly, resulting in a very bitter cup of coffee whereas if it is not packed tightly enough, the result will be weak and watery coffee.

3 Remember that the first coffee through the espresso machine is always the best. Just a few spoonfuls of almost black coffee, followed by the nutty brown froth, or crema, is all that you want. Carry on too long and the coffee will be bitter. Serve immediately.

Variations

Café Latte is a long, milky espresso drink. The standard Italian blend for the brew is equal parts of espresso, milk, and foam, which works well in a cup of not more than 6 fluid ounces, but in a larger mug or beaker that mixture will not hold. So for a standard 12 fluid ounce measure, use half and half espresso and steamed milk, and then top the coffee off with just a thin layer of froth.

Café Americano is espresso diluted with just enough hot water to make a regular cup of coffee.
Café Mocha is the hot fudge sundae of espresso drinks—coffee with chocolate syrup and steamed milk, topped with whipped cream and then decorated with grated or flaked chocolate.
Ristretto is a double-strength, standard espresso, made by switching off the machine sooner so that the coffee is denser.

Classic Cappuccino

Cappuccino is espresso coffee *topped with foamed milk.* **Sweeter than espresso, it is often** *ordered at the end of a meal* **in place of dessert. Most espresso machines incorporate** *a nozzle for frothing milk* **for cappuccinos. Some plunger pots are also adapted to froth milk.** *Serve in large coffee cups.*

Commercially ground fine coffee (allow 1½ to 2 Tbsp per cup)
Water, as required
Milk (allow about 2 fl oz per person)
Nutmeg, cinnamon, cocoa or chocolate powder, to taste
Sugar, to taste

1 Make the espresso according to the instructions on page 15. At the same time heat the milk for the cappuccino. Use a stainless steel jug for this. Pour fresh milk into the jug and place the machine nozzle right inside. Hold the jug handle with one hand and place your other hand underneath the jug.

2 Switch on the machine and wait for the coffee to froth. Once you feel that the milk is warm enough underneath the jug, switch off and remove the jug from the machine. Leave to stand for a few seconds. Pour a little milk into the espresso to sweeten the taste or you will have a bitter cappuccino.

3 Finally, scoop the froth from the top of the milk with a tablespoon. (The best cappuccinos are very frothy.) Sprinkle with nutmeg, cinnamon, cocoa or chocolate powder, or leave plain. Serve immediately.

TIP The milk used for cappuccino-making can be re-heated several times so once the jug has cooled down, leave it, covered, in the refrigerator.

Traditional Tea

For the best cup of breakfast tea, *use loose leaf tea* **that has been carefully stored,** *a china teapot,* **and china cups or mugs.** *Popular teas for breakfast* **include Earl Grey, English Breakfast, Assam, and Ceylon blends.** *Serve plain with a slice of lemon* **or with milk and sugar.**

Cold water
Loose leaf tea (allow 1 tsp per person and one for the pot)
Slices of lemon, or milk and sugar, to taste

1 Fill the kettle with freshly drawn cold water from the faucet or, better still, from a filter jug. Bring to a boil.

2 When the water is almost at a boil, pour a little into the teapot. Swirl it around to warm the pot and then pour it away.

3 Place the tea inside the teapot and then pour boiling water onto the leaves. (Do not allow the kettle to boil for too long.) If you are making white or green tea, use water at a temperature of between 158°F and 203°F, not boiling.

4 Place the lid on the pot and leave to brew for the correct number of minutes according to the manufacturer's instructions on the type of leaf. If you are using an infuser, lift this out of the teapot as soon as the infusion has reached the desired strength. Alternatively, decant the liquor into a second warmed pot. This separates the liquid from the tea leaves and avoids a bitter taste developing.

5 Serve immediately with slices of lemon, or milk and sugar.

TIP Store your tea in an airtight caddy (not made of glass) in a cool, dry place away from any strong-smelling foods and other products. Remember that tea absorbs other flavors very easily.

Breakfast Citrus

This juice is creamy and a *pale orange-yellow in color* **with a tangy, zesty flavor. It is a** *good internal and skin cleanser.*

makes approx. 1 cup

2 large oranges
1 lemon
1 lime
Orange slices to decorate

1 Peel the fruits leaving some white pith. Remove the pits, if preferred, and blend or juice. Alternatively, if you are using a citrus presser or juicer, simply halve the fruits, and then juice.

2 Serve in chilled glasses decorated with orange slices.

TIP For a professional garnish, use a citrus zester to make swirls of peel.

Exotic Fruit

An ideal pick-me-up *for breakfast time, this drink has a* *sweet, refreshing flavor.* **It is also good for the digestive system.**

makes approx. 2¼ cups

½ medium-size pineapple
1 small or "mini" mango
1 Chinese gooseberry

1 Peel the pineapple and chop roughly. Next, peel the mango and slice the flesh away from the pit. Peel the skin from the kiwi fruit. Reserve a small portion of each fruit.

2 Blend all the fruits together and serve sprinkled with chopped fruit. Use a long-handled sundae spoon to eat the fruit from the glass.

Banana Breakfast Milk

This energizing drink is *quick to make and full of flavor.* The rich potassium supply in bananas *gives a real boost* to the body's maintenance program.

makes 2 servings

1¼ cups cold milk
1 small banana
1 Tbsp sugar
2 Tbsp extra-thick heavy
*   cream or yogurt*
Grated nutmeg, banana
*   slices, to decorate*

1 Place the cold milk and cream or yogurt in a blender. Peel the banana, slice, and add to the mixture with the sugar. Process for 1 minute and divide between two glasses.

2 Chill and serve plain or with grated nutmeg and banana slices.

Peach Breakfast Milk

Peaches contain a *good supply of vitamins and minerals.* Choose deep-colored fruits that give a little when pressed. *Wake and shake* with this fragrant drink!

makes 2 to 3 servings

3 small peaches
1¼ cups milk
1 Tbsp superfine sugar
Grated chocolate, to decorate

1 Skin, halve, and pit the peaches. Cut each one into four and place in a blender with the remaining ingredients. Process until smooth.

2 Chill and serve plain, or with a little grated chocolate on top.

Raspberry and Melon Yogurt Drink

Melons and raspberries *are rich sources of vitamins* **B and C. Choose ripe, firm fruits that are unbruised for this refreshing,** *uplifting drink.*

makes 4 generous servings

2½ cups yogurt
8 ice cubes
2 egg whites (see page 7)
1 cup diced, ripe Cantaloupe
1¼ cups raspberries
Sugar, to taste
Raspberries, mint leaves, to
  decorate

Blend all the ingredients together until the ice is crushed. Serve immediately in chilled tall glasses, garnished with raspberries and 1 or 2 mint leaves.

TIP Variations on this recipe are easy to make. Instead of the melon, try any of the following: 2 peaches, peeled and sliced, 3 slices canned pineapple, or 1 mango, sliced, or 1 to 1½ cups of strawberries, blackberries, blueberries, or black currants.

Pear and Blueberry Lassi

makes 2 servings

1 pear
1 cup blueberries
¾ cup low-fat, unsweetened,
  "live" yogurt
2 Tbsp freshly-squeezed lemon
  juice

Traditionally made without fruit *to accompany a rich Indian meal,* **this version adds pear to sweeten naturally and makes a refreshing breakfast drink.** *It has a fragrant flavor,* **and is low in fat and** *good for the digestion.*

1 Wash the pear, peel and core. Place in a blender. Wash the blueberries thoroughly and add them to the pear.

2 Add yogurt and lemon juice. Blend well until smooth and serve in chilled glasses.

Pear and Blueberry Lassi ▶

Fruits
and
Cereals

Exotic Muesli

This delicious breakfast cereal *can be varied* **according to the availability of fruit and nuts. Try substituting** *pineapple, papaya, watermelon, and pecan or hazelnuts.*

makes 4 to 6 servings

6 Tbsp thick yogurt
6 Tbsp rolled oats
1 large mango
2 bananas
3 Chinese gooseberries
2 Tbsp brown sugar
1 Tbsp Brazil nuts, chopped

1 Place the yogurt in a bowl with the oats. Peel the mango and slice the flesh away from the pit. Chop fine and add to the bowl.

2 Peel and slice the bananas and Chinese gooseberries, and add to the bowl. Sprinkle with brown sugar and chopped nuts.

Breakfast Crunch

Packed with flavor and *full of vitamins,* **this breakfast cereal can be** *partly made up in advance* **to save time in the mornings.** *Roast the seeds and pine kernels,* **and store them in airtight containers** *ready for use.*

makes 4 servings

¼ cup sunflower seeds
¼ cup pine kernels
¼ cup sesame seeds
2 oranges
2 Tbsp brown sugar
½ cup dried figs, chopped
2 large bananas
2½ cups Greek yogurt

1 Using a dry skillet, roast the sunflower seeds and pine nuts for 3 minutes over a moderate heat. Add the sesame seeds and roast for a further 3 minutes, stirring to give an even browning. Remove the pan from the heat and leave to cool.

2 Coarsely grate the rind from 1 orange and add to the pan with the sugar and dried figs. Stir until thoroughly combined and cook for 2 minutes. Leave to cool.

3 Remove the rind and pith from the oranges and cut them into pieces. Slice the bananas and mix with the oranges and yogurt. Divide among four dishes and top each with the fig mixture. Serve at once.

Apricot Yogurt Crunch

A variation on a Scottish dish, crunchy oatmeal, spicy yogurt, and *lightly poached fruit* make an attractive morning dish.

makes 4 servings

10 oz apricots, pitted
⅔ cup water
3 Tbsp honey
⅔ cup oatmeal, toasted
½ to 1 tsp ground ginger
1¼ cups low-fat plain yogurt

1 Place the apricots in a pan with the water and 1 tablespoon of the honey. Cook gently for 5 minutes until softened, and drain.

2 Mix the oatmeal and remaining honey in a bowl. Stir the ginger into the yogurt.

3 Alternately layer the fruit, yogurt, and oatmeal mixtures into serving glasses. Chill and serve.

Banana Bran Energy

If you can't face *a full breakfast in the morning,* get your energy from this nutritious dish *drizzled with honey.*

makes 4 servings

1 cup banana slices
*   (2 medium-size fruits)*
Grated rind and juice of
*   1 lemon*
⅔ cup sour cream or yogurt
⅓ cup pecans, chopped rough
1 Tbsp honey
¼ cup bran
Milk

1 Toss the banana slices in lemon juice, then place them in a bowl and carefully mix in the cream or yogurt, nuts, honey, and bran. If the mixture is very thick, add 1 or 2 tablespoons of milk to thin it down.

2 Decorate with the lemon rind just before serving. If serving immediately, a little extra honey may be drizzled over the cream in a zigzag pattern.

Banana Bran Energy ▶

Raspberry Oatie

A deliciously crunchy breakfast *that can be served either hot or cold* **with yogurt.**

makes 4 servings

2¼ cups raspberries
1 Tbsp superfine sugar
¾ stick butter
1½ Tbsp soft brown sugar
¾ cup quick-cook porridge oats
Yogurt, to serve

1 Preheat the oven to 425°F. Divide the raspberries into four individual ovenproof dishes and sprinkle each one with a little superfine sugar.

2 Melt the butter and brown sugar in a saucepan and stir in the oats. Cook for 2 to 3 minutes and then divide among each portion of raspberries, spreading the mixture evenly with a fork.

3 Place in the oven for 10 minutes and then serve either hot or cold with yogurt.

Strawberries with Melon and Orange

This light and refreshing breakfast salad is the *perfect start*
to hot summer days.

makes 4 servings

3 cups halved strawberries
1 small melon, balled
2 oranges
¼ cup orange juice (optional)
Mint leaves

1 Place the halved strawberries in a bowl with the melon balls. Peel the oranges, remove the pits and break into segments, then cut them in half or chop them roughly, depending on size.

2 Add the oranges to the other fruits with any juices, adding extra orange juice if necessary.

3 Leave to stand for 30 minutes. Serve the salad at room temperature, decorated with fresh mint leaves.

Warm Spiced Pears

The aroma from this dish is *almost as good as the taste,* **and all part of the enjoyment. If liked, serve with** *a spoonful of plain yogurt or cottage cheese.*

makes 4 servings

4 large ripe pears, peeled,
halved, and cored
1¼ cups mango juice
1 cinnamon stick, crushed
½ tsp grated nutmeg
3 Tbsp raisins
2 Tbsp granulated brown
sugar

1 Place the pear halves in a pan with the fruit juice, spices, raisins, and sugar. Heat gently to dissolve the sugar and then gradually bring to a boil.

2 Reduce the heat to a simmer and cook for a further 10 minutes until the pears are softened. Serve warm with the syrup.

Broiled Pink Grapefruit

A quick and simple breakfast. *Although speedy to prepare,* **the results are sensational.**

makes 4 servings

2 Florida pink grapefruit
2 Tbsp honey
Pinch of ground allspice
Mint sprigs, to garnish
(optional)

1 Cut the rind away from the grapefruit, remove any remaining pith, and cut each grapefruit into quarters. Place in a heatproof shallow dish.

2 Mix together the honey and allspice, and spoon over the grapefruit pieces. Cook under the broiler for 5 minutes. Serve garnished with mint, if desired.

Warm Spiced Pears ▶

Breakfast
Eggs

Ham "n" Egg Cocottes

**These light savories are *perfect for a special breakfast*.
Shredded Gruyère cheese can be used in place of the Brie.**

makes 4 servings

¼ cup ham, sliced fine
1 Tbsp butter
1½ cups button mushrooms,
*   wiped and sliced*
Freshly ground black pepper
4 medium eggs
4 Tbsp heavy cream
¾ cup Brie cheese, cubed
Warm crusty bread, to serve

Variations

Use 3 skinned, seeded, and chopped tomatoes in place of the mushrooms and sauté them gently for 1 minute. Or use 1 small onion, peeled and chopped, and sauté for 4 to 5 minutes or until softened.

1 Preheat the oven to 375°F for 10 minutes before baking. Cut the ham into strips and use it to line four ramekin dishes. Melt the butter in a small skillet and gently sauté the mushrooms for 2 minutes, drain on paper towels and place in the ramekin dishes. Season with the black pepper.

2 Break an egg into each dish, then pour over 1 tablespoon of the cream. Dot with the cubed cheese. Place in a roasting pan half filled with boiling water, then bake in the preheated oven for about 15 to 20 minutes or until set to personal preference. Serve with warm crusty bread.

Smokie Scramble

Try Parma ham *in place of smoked salmon* **or** *add one roasted bell pepper,* **skinned and chopped, to the egg mixture at the end of cooking time,** *for a variation.*

makes 4 servings

1 cup smoked salmon
6 medium eggs
6 Tbsp light cream
Salt and freshly ground black
*   pepper*
1 Tbsp butter
2 Tbsp chives, chopped fine
Buttered toast or warm sliced
*   brioche, to serve*

1 Cut 1 ounce of the smoked salmon into small strips and reserve. Beat the eggs with the cream and seasoning to taste. Melt the butter in a skillet, then pour the eggs into the skillet and cook very slowly, stirring gently. As the mixture starts to thicken, stir in the salmon strips and 1 tablespoon of chives. Cook until lightly scrambled.

2 Arrange the remaining smoked salmon onto four warmed plates and top with scrambled egg. Sprinkle with the remaining chives and serve with either hot buttered toast or warm sliced brioche and Bucks Fizz (see recipe below).

Bucks Fizz

makes 4 servings

1 cup freshly squeezed orange juice,
*   chilled*
1 bottle non-vintage champagne,
*   chilled*

Pour ¼ cup of orange juice into each of four champagne flutes. Top up with champagne and serve immediately.

Omelet Fines Herbes

Full of nutrition, this omelet is a *classic breakfast recipe*. It can be adapted and *served in various ways* (see Variations).

makes 1 serving

2 medium eggs
Salt and freshly ground black
  pepper
1 Tbsp herbs, chopped fresh,
  such as parsley, chervil,
  tarragon, and chives
1 Tbsp water
1 Tbsp butter, unsalted

1 Lightly whisk the eggs with seasoning to taste until frothy. Stir in the chopped herbs and water.

2 Melt the butter in a skillet, tilting the skillet so that the base is evenly coated with butter. Pour in the beaten eggs and stir gently with a fork, drawing the mixture from the sides of the pan to the center.

3 When the egg has set, stop stirring and cook for a further minute. Then, with a palette knife, fold over a third of the omelet to the center, then fold over the opposite side. Gently slide the omelet onto a warmed plate and serve immediately. Do not overcook otherwise the omelet will be tough.

Variations

If liked, alternative fillings can be used. Try the following: ¼ cup grated cheese stirred into the eggs when the base has set or ¾ cup wiped mushrooms, sliced and lightly sautéed. Alternatively, try ¼ cup shredded ham or 2 tomatoes, skinned and seeded, then chopped or 1 cup cooked peeled shrimp. For a combo dish, place the mushrooms, ham, tomatoes, and shrimp in the center of the omelet after it has set. Cook for 1 to 2 minutes to heat through, then fold over and serve. Sprinkle with a little parsley, chopped fine, as garnish.

Soufflé Omelet

An elegant and *tasty recipe* that can be served at breakfast or as *a light appetizer.*

makes 1 serving

4 oz smoked haddock fillet
½ cup milk
1 bay leaf
1 shallot, peeled and sliced
4 black peppercorns
2 medium eggs, separated
Freshly ground black pepper
1 Tbsp light cream
1 Tbsp butter, unsalted
1 Tbsp Parmesan cheese, grated
Parsley sprigs, to garnish

1 Place the haddock in a skillet with the milk, bay leaf, shallot, and peppercorns. Bring to a boil, then simmer gently for 5 to 8 minutes or until cooked. Drain, cool, then discard the fish skin and bones, and flake.

2 Place the egg yolks in one bowl and the whites in a separate one. Beat the egg yolks with the pepper and cream. Whisk the egg whites until stiff, then gently fold them into the egg yolk mixture.

3 Melt the butter in a clean skillet, tilting the pan so that the base is evenly coated with melted butter. Pour in the egg mixture and cook gently for 2 to 3 minutes or until the base has set. Place the flaked haddock on top and sprinkle with the grated cheese.

4 Place under a preheated broiler and cook under moderate heat until golden on top. Gently ease round the edge of the omelet with a spatula, fold in half, and serve garnished with parsley.

Eggs Florentine

This classic breakfast recipe *can also serve four as a supper dish.*
**If you want to vary the recipe, add 1½ cups of lightly sautéed
mushrooms to the spinach after chopping** *or place three sliced tomatoes
on top of the spinach* **before arranging the halved eggs in the dish.**

makes 8 servings as a light breakfast

8 medium eggs
*1 lb fresh spinach, tough
    stalks discarded and well
    washed*
4 Tbsp butter
*1 small onion, peeled and
    chopped fine*
*1 to 2 garlic cloves, peeled
    and crushed*

for the cheese sauce

⅓ cup all-purpose white flour
1 cup milk
1 tsp Dijon mustard
*Salt and freshly ground black
    pepper*
¼ cup Gruyère cheese, grated
Warm crusty bread, to serve

1 Preheat the broiler to medium. Place the eggs in a pan, cover with cold water, and bring to a boil. Boil gently for 10 minutes, then plunge the eggs into cold water. Leave until cold, peel, and cut in half.

2 Meanwhile, rinse the spinach thoroughly then place in a pan with just the water clinging to their leaves. Cover with a lid and cook for 3 to 4 minutes, drain, and chop fine.

3 Heat 1 tablespoon of the butter in a small pan and gently sauté the onion and garlic for 5 minutes or until softened. Stir in the chopped spinach, then place in the base of an ovenproof gratin dish. Place the halved boiled eggs on top.

4 Melt the remaining butter in a small pan, then stir in the flour and cook for 2 minutes. Draw off the heat and gradually stir in the milk. Return to the heat and cook, stirring until the mixture thickens and coats the back of a spoon. Remove and stir in the mustard, seasoning, and half the grated cheese. Pour over the eggs, sprinkle with the remaining cheese, and place under the broiler for 8 to 10 minutes or until golden brown and bubbly. Serve immediately with warm crusty bread.

Eggs Benedict

To vary *this traditional favorite,* **replace the asparagus spears with strips of skinned bell pepper or** *lightly sautéed strips of zucchini.*

makes 4 servings

for the hollandaise sauce

2 Tbsp wine vinegar
1 Tbsp water
2 medium egg yolks
1 stick butter
Salt and freshly ground black pepper

for the eggs benedict

4 medium eggs
6 to 8 oz asparagus spears
4 slices white or whole-wheat bread
4 slices of ham
1 Tbsp parsley, freshly chopped

1 Place the vinegar and water in a small pan and boil vigorously until reduced by half, then cool. Place the egg yolks in a basin over a pan of gently simmering water and stir in the vinegar mixture. Heat gently, stirring throughout, until the mixture thickens.

2 Divide the butter into small portions, then whisk in one portion at a time until the sauce coats the back of a wooden spoon. Add seasoning to taste. If the sauce is too sharp, whisk in a little more butter.

3 While the sauce is cooling, poach the eggs either in an egg poacher or in a skillet filled with gently simmering water (see Hot Tips for Perfect Eggs, page 10). Trim the asparagus spears and lightly steam in an asparagus steamer or cook gently in a skillet in simmering water for 6 to 8 minutes or until tender. Drain and reserve.

4 Toast the bread on both sides, then fold the ham in half, and place on top of the toast. Top with the asparagus spears and then place a poached egg on top. Spoon over the hollandaise sauce and garnish with parsley sprigs. Serve immediately.

Crispy Breakfast Cups

If you want to vary this recipe for a brunch dish, *replace the mushrooms* **with 2 ounces asparagus, lightly cooked and chopped,** *or try 2 ounces broccoli flowerets,* **lightly cooked and refreshed.**

makes 4 servings

8 square slices bread, white or whole-wheat
6 Tbsp melted butter
1 cup button mushrooms, wiped and sliced
4 medium eggs
2 Tbsp light cream
Salt and freshly ground black pepper
¼ cup ham, chopped fine
2 Tbsp chives, chopped

1 Preheat the oven to 400°F. Trim the crusts from the bread and brush both sides of the bread with 4 tablespoons of the melted butter. Place the bread diagonally into individual muffin or patty pans so that the corners stick up. Bake in the preheated oven for 12 to 15 minutes or until crisp. Keep warm until ready to use.

2 Cook the mushrooms in the remaining butter for 2 minutes; drain and reserve.

Whisk the eggs with the cream and seasoning to taste. Heat the remaining butter, then pour in the eggs, and cook gently, stirring well throughout for 3 to 4 minutes. Stir in the mushrooms and ham, and continue to cook for 1 to 2 minutes or until lightly scrambled.

3 Fill the crispy bread cups with the scramble mixture, sprinkle with chives, and serve immediately.

Brunch-style Croque

For a variation to this recipe, **use a softer cheese in place of the** **Gruyère** *– try Chaume or Port Salut.*

makes 4 servings

8 slices bacon
4 slices white or whole-wheat
*   bread*
Butter for spreading
4 oz Gruyère cheese, sliced
3 tomatoes
1 Tbsp olive oil
4 medium eggs

1 Preheat the broiler and broil the bacon for 5 to 6 minutes or until cooked. Drain and reserve. Lightly toast the bread and spread with butter. Top with the cheese and place under the broiler. Cook gently for 5 minutes or until golden.

2 Slice the tomatoes and place on top of the cheese, then top with the bacon. Meanwhile, heat the oil in a skillet, break in the eggs, and fry them for 3 to 4 minutes. Baste the eggs with oil so that they cook evenly on top and underneath. Drain and place an egg on each slice of toast and serve immediately.

Breads *and* Cakes

Chocolate-chip and Peanut-butter Bread

This is a moist, dense bread *with a good flavor.* **The chocolate-crumb topping is** *similar to a famous chocolate candy.*

makes 8 to 10 servings

2 cups all-purpose flour
2 tsp baking powder
¼ tsp salt
1 cup semisweet chocolate chips
¾ cup smooth or chunky peanut butter, at room temperature
1 Tbsp sugar
1 egg, lightly beaten
1 cup milk
1 tsp vanilla extract

for the chocolate-crumb topping

½ cup sugar
¼ cup unsweetened cocoa powder
3 Tbsp unsalted butter, cut into pieces
2 Tbsp dry-roasted peanuts, chopped fine

1 Preheat the oven to 350°F. Lightly grease or spray an 9 x 5-inch loaf pan. Sift the flour, baking powder, and salt into a large bowl. Stir in the chocolate chips, and make a well in the center.

2 Put the peanut butter, sugar, the egg, milk, and vanilla extract in another bowl and beat with an electric mixer. Pour into the well, and lightly stir with a fork until combined.

3 Combine the crumb-topping ingredients in a small bowl. Spoon half the batter into the prepared pan and smooth the top, sprinkling with half of the crumb mixture. Spoon the remaining batter into the pan and gently smooth the top. Sprinkle with the remaining crumb mixture. Using a round-bladed knife or spoon handle, gently draw through the batter in a zigzag pattern to marbelize the mixture slightly.

4 Bake until risen and golden, and a cake tester inserted in the center comes out moist, but with no uncooked crumbs attached, 50 to 55 minutes. Remove to a wire rack to cool, about 25 minutes, then carefully unmold onto a wire rack, top-side up. Cool completely, then wrap and keep for 1 day before serving, if possible.

Whole-wheat Morning Rolls

The dough *can be made overnight* **to make creamy, soft rolls in time for breakfast. There is nothing better than waking up to** *the smell of freshly baked bread* **– a marvelous way to impress your guests.**

makes 18 rolls

for the overnight dough

2½ cups warm water
3 cups whole-wheat bread
*   flour*
1 Tbsp salt
1 package active-dry yeast

for the morning dough

1 package active-dry yeast
¾ cup warm water
3½ cups whole-wheat bread
*   flour*
¼ cup margarine
1 tsp light brown sugar

1 Place the water for the overnight dough in a large bowl. Add the flour, salt, and yeast and mix lightly – do not beat or knead. Cover the dough with a clean kitchen towel and leave overnight at room temperature.

2 In the morning, add all the remaining ingredients to the bowl and mix to a manageable dough; the margarine will be incorporated during the mixing. Turn out onto a floured surface and knead well for about 10 minutes until smooth and elastic.

3 Divide the dough into 18 pieces and shape them into rolls. Place on lightly greased cookie sheets, quite close together so that they grow into each other and form a broken crust. Cover and leave in a warm place for 30 minutes to rise.

4 Preheat the oven to 425°F. Bake the rolls for about 20 minutes. The bases will sound hollow when tapped, but the tops of the rolls will only brown slightly and remain soft. Cool on a wire rack and serve with one of the delicious homemade Preserves, Butters, and Spreads on pages 12 and 13.

Cranberry-apricot-banana Bread
with Cranberry-apricot Compote

The flavors of this *moist, delicious tea bread* are accentuated by the *Cranberry-apricot Compote*, a quick, warm preserve.

makes 18 rolls

1¼ cups all-purpose flour
1½ tsp baking powder
½ tsp freshly grated or ground nutmeg
½ cup old-fashioned oats
1 cup firmly packed, light-brown sugar
½ cup dried cranberries
½ cup dried apricots, chopped
2 eggs
½ cup sunflower or vegetable oil
1 tsp vanilla extract
2 ripe bananas, mashed

for glaze (optional)

¼ cup confectioners' sugar
2 to 3 Tbsp lemon juice or water

1 Preheat the oven to 350°F. Lightly grease and flour a 8 x 4-inch loaf pan. Sift the flour, baking powder, and nutmeg into a bowl. Stir in the oats, brown sugar, cranberries, and apricots until well blended, and make a well in the center.

2 Using an electric mixer in a medium bowl, beat the eggs, oil, vanilla extract, and mashed bananas until well blended. Pour into the well and stir until combined. Scrape the batter into the prepared pan, smoothing the top evenly.

3 Bake until well risen and golden brown, and a cake tester inserted in the center comes out with just a crumb or two attached, about 1 hour. Remove to a wire rack to cool, about 10 minutes, then unmold top-side up onto the rack to cool completely.

4 If glazing, in a small bowl stir the confectioners' sugar and 2 to 3 tablespoons lemon juice until it reaches a pouring consistency. Add a little more lemon juice or water if necessary. Drizzle over the top of the tea bread and allow to set. Alternatively, dust with confectioners' sugar. Serve slices with the Cranberry-apricot Compote.

Cranberry-apricot Compote

makes about 2 cups

½ cup fresh or frozen cranberries
½ cup dried cranberries
10 to 12 oz dried, "no soak" apricots, chopped
½ cup sugar
1 cinnamon stick
Grated rind and juice of 1 orange
2 Tbsp ruby port or marsala wine
1 tsp vanilla extract

Put the dried fruits, sugar, cinnamon stick, grated orange rind and juice in a medium heavy-based, noncorrosive saucepan. Add enough water to cover the fruit. Place over medium heat, and bring to a boil. Simmer over low heat until the cranberries pop, the fruits are tender, and almost all the liquid is absorbed. Remove from the heat, discard the cinnamon stick, and stir in the port or marsala and vanilla. Pour into a bowl and serve warm, or refrigerate, covered, until ready to serve.

Honey-walnut Bread

This dense, nutty, slightly sweet bread is delicious for breakfast, especially with *soft cheeses.*

makes 1 loaf

1½ cups water
1 Tbsp sugar
2 cups whole-wheat flour
1½ cups all-purpose flour
2½ tsp salt
2 Tbsp honey
Water
1 package active-dry yeast
1 cup walnut halves, chopped,
  plus extra walnut halves
  for decoration (optional)
1 egg, lightly beaten, for
  glazing

1 In a small saucepan gently heat the water and sugar until very warm (120°F to 130°F). In a large bowl, stir the whole-wheat flour, all-purpose flour, and salt together until well blended, and make a well in the center. Stir the honey into the warm water and pour into the well. Sprinkle the yeast over it and allow to stand until foamy, about 15 minutes.

2 Pour in the remaining water, and slowly incorporate the flour from the edge of the well into the liquid with an electric mixer on low speed or a wooden spoon, mixing to form a smooth dough. If the dough is very sticky, sprinkle in a little more flour.

3 Turn dough onto a lightly floured surface, and knead until smooth and elastic, about 5 minutes. Place the dough in a greased bowl, turning to grease the top. Cover with a clean dish towel or plastic bag and leave to rise in a warm place (80°F to 85°F) until doubled in volume, about 1½ hours.

4 Grease a large cookie sheet. Punch down the dough and turn onto a lightly floured surface. Sprinkle over the chopped walnuts, and knead into the dough until evenly distributed. Shape the dough into a round or oval, and place on the cookie sheet. Cover with a dish towel and leave in a warm place to rise again until just doubled in volume, about ½ hour.

5 Preheat the oven to 425°F. Brush the loaf with the egg glaze. With a sharp knife, slash the top of the dough in 3 to 4 places and bake for 15 minutes. Reduce the oven temperature to 375°F, and bake until the loaf is deep-golden brown, about 40 minutes more. Remove to a wire rack, sliding the loaf onto the rack to cool completely. Serve warm with soft cheeses.

Sticky Cinnamon Buns
with brown sugar-butter topping

These buns are topped with *a tasty sugar-butter mixture* that caramelizes as they bake.

makes 18 buns

1 cup milk
1 stick butter or margarine
½ cup sugar
1 tsp salt
1 package active-dry yeast
4 to 4½ cups all-purpose
*   flour*
2 eggs, lightly beaten
2 tsp vanilla extract
1 tsp ground cinnamon

brown sugar-butter topping

1½ cups firmly packed,
*   dark-brown sugar*
¼ stick butter
⅔ cup water
2 tsp ground cinnamon
¼ cup chopped pecans
3 Tbsp sugar
¼ cup raisins

TIP To check if the dough has doubled in volume press a finger into the dough. If the hole remains, the dough is ready to be punched down.

1 Put the milk and butter into a saucepan and heat over low heat until very warm. Meanwhile, stir the sugar, salt, yeast, and 1 cup flour together in a large bowl, and make a well in the center.

2 Pour the warm milk into the well, and gradually beat with an electric mixer on low speed, until well blended. Beat in the eggs, vanilla extract, cinnamon, and 1 cup more of the flour, and continue beating for a further 2 minutes. With a wooden spoon, stir in 2 more cups of flour until a soft dough forms.

3 Turn the dough onto a lightly floured surface, and knead until smooth and elastic, about 10 minutes. Shape the dough into a ball, and place in a greased bowl, turning to grease the top. Cover with a clean dish towel, and leave to rise in a warm place (80°F to 85°F), about 2 hours.

4 Meanwhile, prepare the topping. Put the brown sugar, butter, water, and half the cinnamon in a saucepan, and heat over low heat until the sugar dissolves and the butter is melted. Bring to a boil, and simmer until syrupy, about 8 minutes. Pour about 1 tablespoon of the syrup into the bottom of 18 regular muffin-pan cups. Sprinkle in a little of the chopped pecans, sugar, and raisins into each cup.

5 Punch down the dough and place on a lightly floured surface, and roll into a rectangle, about 18 x 12 inches. Sprinkle evenly with the remaining pecans, sugar, raisins, and cinnamon. Beginning with a long side, roll the dough jelly-roll style to form a log. With a sharp knife, cut into eighteen 1-inch slices, and place each slice in a prepared muffin-pan cup, cut-side up. Cover and leave to rise, about 45 minutes.

6 Preheat the oven to 375°F. Bake until risen and well colored, about 25 minutes. Remove muffin pans from the oven, and invert onto a jelly-roll pan; do not remove the muffin-pan cups, but allow each to cool for 3 minutes. Remove the muffin pans. Transfer buns to the rack to cool; serve warm, sticky-side up.

Apricot-filled Danish Ring

This luxurious coffeecake is filled with a purée of dried apricots and *drizzled with a lemon-sugar glaze* – a classic for coffee mornings.

makes 10 to 12 servings

½ cup water
¼ cup sugar
1 package active-dry yeast
2½ cups all-purpose flour
1 tsp salt
1 egg, lightly beaten
½ tsp vanilla extract
½ tsp almond extract
2 sticks unsalted butter
1 egg yolk, beaten with 1 Tbsp
*   water, for glazing*
Slivered almonds, for
*   sprinkling*

apricot filling

1 cup dried, "no-soak"
*   apricots*
2 Tbsp butter, softened
2 Tbsp honey or sugar to taste
Grated rind of 1 lemon plus
*   1 Tbsp lemon juice*
½ tsp almond extract
1 to 2 Tbsp apricot preserves

lemon-sugar glaze

½ cup confectioners' sugar
2 to 3 Tbsp lemon juice

1 Heat the water and 1 tablespoon sugar until very warm (120°F to 130°F). Pour into a bowl and sprinkle over the yeast; allow to stand until foamy, about 15 minutes. Stir the flour, remaining sugar, and salt to blend, and make a well in the center. Whisk the egg, vanilla, and almond extracts into the yeast mixture and pour into the well. Stir until a rough dough forms. Place on a lightly floured surface, and knead well until smooth, about 5 minutes. Cover in plastic wrap and refrigerate for about 10 minutes.

2 Put the butter between 2 sheets of plastic wrap and roll into a rectangular shape. Fold the butter in half and roll out again. Repeat until butter is smooth and pliable, but still cold. Flatten to form a 6 x 4-inch rectangle. On a lightly floured surface roll the dough to an 18 x 8-inch rectangle, keeping the center third thicker than the two outer ends. Put the butter rectangle on the thicker center of the dough and fold the bottom third of the dough over the butter. Fold the top third of the dough over the bottom to enclose the butter; press down the "open edges" to seal the dough to create a neat dough "package."

3 Turn the dough "package" so that the short "open edge" faces you and the folded edge is on the left. Gently roll the dough to a rectangle about 18 inches long, keeping the edges straight; do not press out the butter. Fold the rectangle in thirds, as for enclosing the butter, and press down the edges to seal. Press a finger into one corner to mark the first turn clearly. Wrap the dough tightly and

refrigerate for 30 minutes. Repeat the rolling and folding twice more, wrapping, marking, and chilling the dough between each turn. After the third turn, wrap and refrigerate the dough for 2 hours.

4 For the filling, process all the ingredients until smooth. Grease a large cookie sheet.

5 Soften the dough at room temperature for easier rolling. On a lightly floured surface, roll the dough to form a rectangle of about 28 x 12 inches. Spread the filling to within 1 inch of the edges. Beginning at one long side, fold the dough loosely, about 3 times, jelly-roll style. Transfer to the cookie sheet and bring the two ends together. Brush one end with a little water, and pinch the edges together to seal, forming a ring.

6 Make diagonal snips, perpendicular to the ring and 1½ inches apart, into the outer edge of the ring. Gently pull and twist every other slice of the ring toward the outer edge. Pull and twist the alternating slices toward the center to expose the spiral effect of the filling. Cover and leave in a warm place to rise again until just doubled, approximately 40 minutes.

7 Preheat the oven to 400°F. Brush with the egg glaze and sprinkle with slivered almonds. Bake until golden brown, about 35 minutes. Remove to a wire rack to cool, about 10 minutes. While the ring is still warm, stir the sugar and lemon juice together, then drizzle generously over.

Croissants
and
Brioches

Lemon Brioche Loaf

Rich and buttery, *classic French brioche* is a favorite breakfast treat. *It can be baked in a loaf pan,* but use the traditional molds if you like; be sure to start the dough *the night before you want the loaf.*

makes one 9 x 5-inch loaf

2 Tbsp sugar
3 Tbsp water
1 package active-dry yeast
2 eggs, lightly beaten
1 to 1½ cups all-purpose
*   flour*
¾ tsp salt
Grated rind of 1 lemon
¾ stick unsalted butter, cut
*   into small pieces, softened*
1 egg yolk beaten with 1 Tbsp
*   water, for glazing*

1 Put 1 tablespoon of the sugar in a small saucepan with the water, and heat over low heat until very warm (120°F to 130°F), stirring to dissolve the sugar. Sprinkle over the yeast and allow to stand until yeast is foamy, about 5 to 10 minutes. Stir to dissolve, then beat in the eggs.

2 Put the flour, salt, grated lemon rind, and remaining sugar in a food processor fitted with a metal blade, and blend. With the machine running, slowly pour the yeast-egg mixture through the feed tube; a dough will form immediately. Scrape down the side of the bowl, and process the dough until very well kneaded, 2 to 3 minutes. Sprinkle over the softened butter pieces, and pulse in the butter until just blended, about 12 times.

3 Scrape the dough into a large, greased bowl, turning to grease the top. Cover with a clean dish towel and leave to rise in a warm place (80°F to 85°F) until dough doubles in volume, about 1½ hours. (At this point the dough can be refrigerated overnight to rise very slowly.)

4 Butter a 9 x 5-inch loaf pan. Punch down the dough and turn onto a lightly floured surface; knead lightly 2 to 3 times. Divide the dough into 8 or 9 pieces, and shape into balls. Arrange the dough balls in the pan, pushing them together to fit. Cover and leave to rise in a warm place until just doubled in volume, about 40 minutes.

5 Preheat the oven to 400°F. Brush the top of the risen loaf with the egg glaze and bake until well risen and deep-golden brown, about 30 minutes. Remove to a wire rack, and unmold immediately, top-side up, to cool. Serve warm with butter and homemade preserves (see Preserves, Butters, and Spreads on pages 12 and 13), if desired.

Almond Croissants

These tender, flaky croissants **are filled with a homemade almond paste for an extra-luxurious treat.** *Making them is well worth the effort.*

makes 24 croissants

1⅓ cups milk
2 Tbsp sugar
1 package active-dry yeast
3 to 3½ cups all-purpose flour
1½ tsp salt
2 sticks unsalted butter
1 egg, with 1 tsp water, for glazing
Slivered almonds for sprinkling
Confectioners' sugar, for dusting (optional)

almond paste

⅔ cup blanched almonds
1 Tbsp all-purpose flour
1 Tbsp cornstarch
½ cup sugar
¼ stick unsalted butter, cut into pieces, softened
1 egg
1 egg yolk
½ tsp almond extract

TIP In Step 6, if the butter squeezes out of the package, or the dough becomes sticky at any time, slide it out onto a cookie sheet and chill until easier to handle.

1 In a small saucepan, heat the milk and half of the sugar over low heat until very warm (120°F to 130°F). Pour into the bowl of an electric mixer, and sprinkle over the yeast and 1 tablespoon of the flour. Allow to stand until foamy, about 15 minutes. With a hand whisk, beat in 1 cup of the flour, the salt, and the remaining sugar.

2 Fit the mixer with the dough hook, and gradually beat in 2 cups of flour on low speed. Beat on high until the dough comes together and begins to pull away from the side of the bowl; if the dough is very wet, sprinkle in a little more flour. Beat until smooth. Scrape the dough into a greased bowl. Cover and let rise in a warm place (80°F to 85°F) until dough doubles in volume, about 1½ hours.

3 Punch down the dough and turn onto a lightly floured surface; knead lightly until smooth, 4 to 5 times. Wrap in a dish towel and refrigerate about 10 minutes, while preparing the butter.

4 Put the butter between 2 sheets of plastic wrap, and roll the butter into a rectangular shape. Fold the butter in half and roll out again. Repeat until butter is smooth and pliable, but still cold. Flatten to form a 6 x 4-inch rectangle.

5 Roll the dough to a 18 x 8-inch rectangle on a lightly floured surface, keeping the center third thicker than the two outer ends. Put the butter rectangle on the thicker center of the dough, and fold the bottom third of the dough over the butter. Fold the top third of the dough over the bottom to enclose the butter; with the rolling pin press down the "open edges" to seal the dough and create a neat dough "package."

6 Turn the dough "package" so that the short "open edge" faces you, the folded edge is on the left and it resembles a closed book. Gently roll the dough to a rectangle about 18 inches long, keeping the edges straight; do not press out the butter. Fold the rectangle in thirds, as for enclosing the butter, and press down the edges to seal. Press your index finger into one corner to mark the first turn clearly. Wrap the dough in plastic wrap, and refrigerate for 30 minutes.

7 Repeat the rolling and folding, or "turns," twice more, wrapping, marking, and chilling the dough between each turn. After the third turn, wrap and refrigerate the dough for at least 2 hours.

8 Meanwhile, prepare the almond paste. Put the blanched almonds, flour, cornstarch, and sugar in the bowl of a food processor, and process until very fine crumbs form. Sprinkle over the butter, the egg, egg yolk, and almond extract, and process until a smooth paste forms. If not using immediately, cover and refrigerate.

9 Lightly grease 2 large cookie sheets. Allow the dough to soften at room temperature, about 5 to 10 minutes, for easier rolling.

Roll the dough to a ⅛-inch thick rectangle about 13 inches wide on a lightly floured surface. Trim the edges straight. Cut the rectangle in half to form 2 long, narrow strips. Cut each strip into triangles, 6 inches high and 4 inches wide at the base. With the rolling pin, roll gently from the base to the point, stretching each triangle lengthwise.

10 Place a tablespoon of almond paste about 1 inch up from the base of each triangle. Pulling the base slightly to widen it, roll up the dough from the base to the point. Arrange point-side down on the cookie sheets, curving the ends to form a crescent shape. Brush each croissant with a little egg glaze; cover and leave to rise in a warm place until almost tripled in volume, about 2 hours. (At this point, the formed croissants can be refrigerated overnight and baked the following day, but be sure to refrigerate the egg glaze until ready to bake the croissants.)

11 Preheat the oven to 475°F. Brush each croissant again with the egg glaze, then sprinkle each with a few flaked almonds. Bake for 2 minutes, then reduce the oven temperature to 375°F and bake until a light golden color, approximately 10 minutes more. Remove to a wire rack to cool. Dust lightly with confectioners' sugar, and serve warm with fresh coffee.

Chocolate Croissants

This recipe is always a favorite at breakfast time. *The dough can be made up in advance* **the night before and kept** *chilled in the refrigerator* **to save time.**

makes 12 croissants

4½ cups strong white (bread) flour
1 tsp salt
2 Tbsp lard
1½ Tbsp fresh yeast
1 cup tepid water
1 egg, beaten, and 1 egg for glazing
1½ sticks butter
1 cup chocolate chips
2 tsp water
1 tsp sugar

1 Preheat the oven to 425°F. Sift together the flour and salt. Blend in the lard. Mix the yeast with the water and add the yeast liquid and beaten egg to the flour. Mix thoroughly to a soft dough.

2 Knead lightly on a floured surface for 10 to 15 minutes until smooth. Roll out to a strip 20 x 8 inches. Soften the butter and divide into three. Dot one portion of butter over two-thirds of the dough. Fold the dough in three, folding up the unbuttered portion first. Seal the edge with a rolling pin. Wrap in plastic wrap and chill.

3 Repeat the process twice more, using the other portions of butter. Roll out the dough and fold three more times. Chill for at least one hour. Roll the dough out to a rectangle 22 x 12 inches. Trim the edges and cut in half lengthways. Cut each strip of dough into triangles.

4 At the base end of each triangle, place a little pile of chocolate chips. Beat together the second egg, water, and sugar. Brush over the edges of each croissant. Roll up the croissants loosely, starting at the base and finishing with the tip underneath. Place on a cookie sheet, and shape.

5 Cover with oiled plastic wrap and leave to rise for 20 to 30 minutes. Brush with glaze. Bake in the oven for about 20 minutes. Cool on a wire rack. Serve warm.

Chocolate Poppy-seed Braid

This sweet-yeast dough is *filled with a rich, poppy-seed* **and chocolate-chip mixture before being braided.** *It makes a beautiful addition* **to any breakfast or brunch table.**

makes 12 to 14 servings

¼ *cup water*
¼ *cup sugar*
1 package active-dry yeast
¼ *cup lukewarm milk*
½ *tsp salt*
1 egg, lightly beaten
½ *stick butter, softened*
3 to 3½ cups all-purpose flour
1 egg yolk, beaten with 1 Tbsp milk, for glazing

chocolate poppy-seed filling

¼ *cup poppy seeds*
¼ *cup sugar*
¼ *cup raisins*
½ *tsp ground cinnamon*
Grated rind of ½ orange
¼ *cup sour cream*
1 Tbsp marmalade or apricot preserves
½ *cup semisweet-chocolate chips*

1 In a small saucepan over low heat, heat the water and 1 tablespoon sugar until very warm (120°F to 130°F). Pour into the bowl of a heavy-duty electric mixer, and sprinkle over the yeast. Allow to stand until foamy, about 15 minutes.

2 Fit the mixer with the dough hook and beat in the warm milk, remaining sugar, salt, egg, and butter. On low speed, gradually beat in 3 cups of the flour until a soft dough forms. If the dough is very sticky, add a little more flour. Beat until the dough comes together and becomes elastic.

3 Turn the dough onto a lightly floured surface, and knead until smooth and elastic, 2 to 3 minutes, adding a little more flour if necessary. Place the dough in a greased bowl, turning to grease the top. Cover with a clean dish towel, and let rise in a warm place (80°F to 85°F) until doubled in volume, about 1½ hours.

4 Meanwhile, prepare the filling. Put all the ingredients except the chocolate chips in the bowl of a food processor fitted with the metal blade, and process using the pulse button, until well blended, but not completely smooth. Grease a large cookie sheet.

5 Punch down the dough and turn onto a lightly floured surface, kneading 2 or 3 times. With a lightly floured rolling pin, roll into a rectangle about 15 x 10 inches. To transfer to the cookie sheet, roll the dough

around the rolling pin and carefully unroll onto the cookie sheet, stretching gently to keep the shape. Spread the filling down the center third of the dough, to within about 2 inches from each end.

6 With a sharp knife, cut 8 to 10 diagonal slashes from both sides of the filling to both edges of the dough, cutting about ½ inch from the filling. Beginning at one end, fold the end over the bottom edge of the filling, then fold over all the strips from alternate sides, and tuck the ends of the strips under the braid. Cover with the dish towel, and leave in a warm place to rise again until almost doubled in volume.

7 Preheat the oven to 375°F. Brush the braid with the egg glaze, and bake until golden and well browned, about 30 minutes. Remove the cookie sheet to a wire rack to cool, 15 to 20 minutes, then carefully transfer the braid onto the rack to cool until just warm.

Sweet Polenta Cake
with caramelized apples

This cake is a slightly more upmarket *version of a sweet cornbread* – there are many versions found all over Italy.

makes 6 to 8 servings

¾ cup all-purpose flour
½ cup polenta or yellow
*   cornmeal*
1 tsp baking powder
Grated rind of 1 lemon
¼ tsp salt
2 eggs
¾ cup sugar
⅓ cup milk
½ tsp almond extract
¼ cup currants or raisins,
*   soaked in hot water for 20*
*   minutes, and well drained*
¾ stick unsalted butter,
*   softened*
2 dessert apples, peeled, cored,
*   and thinly sliced*
¼ cup slivered almonds
3 to 4 Tbsp apricot preserve
1 to 2 Tbsp water
Whipped cream or sour
*   cream, to serve (optional)*

1 Preheat the oven to 375°F. Generously butter a 9-inch springform pan, then dust the pan lightly with flour. Stir the flour, polenta, or cornmeal, baking powder, grated lemon rind, and salt together in a large bowl.

2 Beat the eggs and ½ cup of the sugar in another bowl with an electric mixer until foamy; gradually beat in the milk and almond extract. Stir in the drained currants or raisins. Beat in the dry ingredients on low speed, adding 4 tablespoons of the butter.

3 Spoon into the prepared pan and smooth the top evenly. Arrange the apple slices in concentric circles over the top, and sprinkle with the slivered almonds. In a small saucepan, melt the remaining 2 tablespoons of butter over low heat, and drizzle over the apples. Sprinkle with the remaining sugar.

4 Bake until the cake is puffed and golden, and the apples are lightly caramelized, about 45 minutes. Remove to a wire rack to cool, about 20 minutes. Run a thin knife blade between the cake edge and pan side, then unclip the pan side and carefully remove. Heat the apricot preserves with 1 to 2 tablespoons of water in a small saucepan until melted and smooth. Carefully brush or spoon over the top of the apples to glaze. Allow to cool to room temperature, and serve with whipped cream or sour cream, as preferred.

TIP Be sure to stir or sift together the dry ingredients (including any grated or ground spices) until they are thoroughly blended. Most wet ingredients can be beaten until well-blended with a hand whisk or fork. Heavier mixtures that include mashed bananas, pumpkin, or sweet potato might require a hand-held electric mixer.

Muffins

and

Scones

Almond-Poppy seed Muffins

Poppy seeds add a *delicate flavor and slightly crunchy texture*
to these light, almond-flavored muffins.

makes 12 muffins

2 Tbsp poppy seeds, plus
extra for sprinkling
1¼ cups all-purpose flour
2 tsp baking powder
½ tsp salt
½ cup sugar, plus extra for
sprinkling
1 egg
¾ cup milk
¼ cup sunflower or other
light vegetable oil, or
4 Tbsp butter or
margarine, melted and
cooled
½ tsp almond extract
½ cup whole blanched
almonds, lightly toasted
and chopped

1 Preheat the oven to 375°F. Grease or spray a 12-cup muffin pan, or line each cup with paper or foil liners. Put 2 tablespoons of the poppy seeds in a bowl and crush lightly with the back of a spoon. Sift the flour, baking powder, and salt, then stir in the sugar until well blended, and make a well in the center.

2 Beat the eggs and milk together in a bowl or 4-cup measure until well blended. Gradually beat in the oil, melted butter or margarine, and the almond extract. Pour into the well, add the chopped almonds and stir lightly or until just blended. Do not overmix; the batter should be slightly lumpy.

3 Spoon the mixture into the prepared cups, filling each about ¾ full. Combine a tablespoon of sugar and one teaspoon of poppy seeds in a small cup; sprinkle a little mixture over the top of each muffin. Bake until risen and golden, and cake tester inserted into the center comes out clean, 20 to 25 minutes. Remove pan to a wire rack to cool, about 2 minutes, then remove the muffins to a wire rack to cool. Serve warm or at room temperature.

Very Blue-blueberry Muffins

These muffins *are bursting with blueberries;* **mashing some of the berries releases** *more flavor into the batter.*

makes 12 muffins

2 cups all-purpose flour
2½ tsp baking powder
½ tsp salt
¼ tsp freshly grated or ground nutmeg
¾ cup sugar
2 eggs
¾ cup milk
1 stick butter or margarine, melted and cooled
Grated rind of ½ orange
1 tsp vanilla extract
½ cup fresh blueberries, mashed
2 cups fresh blueberries, whole
¼ cup coarse sugar, mixed with ¼ tsp freshly grated nutmeg, for sprinkling

1 Preheat the oven to 375°F. Lightly grease or spray a 12-cup muffin pan or line each cup with a paper liner. Sift the flour, baking powder, salt, and grated nutmeg into a large bowl; stir in the sugar, and make a deep well in the center.

2 In another bowl, beat the eggs, milk, melted butter or margarine, grated orange rind, and vanilla extract; then stir in the mashed blueberries. Pour into the well and lightly stir using a fork, until blended in. Do not overmix. Lightly fold in the remaining whole blueberries.

3 Spoon the batter into the prepared muffin cups, filling each to almost full. Sprinkle each with the sugar-nutmeg mixture, and bake until risen and golden (a cake tester or toothpick inserted in the center should come out with a few crumbs attached), around 25 to 30 minutes. Remove pan to a wire rack to cool, about 2 minutes, then remove muffins to the wire rack to cool. Serve warm or at room temperature.

TIP Muffin pan cups can vary in size, depending on the manufacturer. Your batter may not completely fill each cup; if so, it doesn't really matter.

Walnut-date Scones
with sweet date-butter

These dark, dense scones are *delicious and moist,* **and make a substantial breakfast with** *a bowl of yogurt drizzled with honey.*

makes 8 scones

¾ cup all-purpose flour
¾ cup whole-wheat flour and a little extra for dusting
4 tsp baking powder
½ tsp salt
½ tsp ground cinnamon
¼ cup firmly packed, light-brown sugar
¼ stick butter, cut into pieces
½ cup chopped walnuts, lightly toasted
½ cup chopped dates
½ to ¾ cup milk

Sweet Date-Butter

makes about 1 cup

2 sticks unsalted butter
1 cup chopped, pitted dates
1 to 2 tbsp honey
½ tsp ground cardamom or cinnamon

1 Preheat the oven to 425°F. Lightly flour a large cookie sheet. Sift the flours, baking powder, salt, and cinnamon into a large bowl; stir in the brown sugar.

2 Sprinkle the butter pieces over the flour, and blend in the butter using a pastry blender or your fingertips, until the mixture resembles coarse crumbs. Stir in the walnuts and dates, and make a well in the center. Add ½ cup milk and stir lightly until a soft dough forms, adding a little more milk if necessary. Form into a rough ball.

3 Place on a lightly floured surface and knead once or twice. Roll out or pat into a ¾-inch-thick square. Using a sharp knife dipped in flour, cut straight down into 8 to 9 squares, but do not drag the knife or the scones will rise unevenly. Transfer the scones to the cookie sheet, arranging them about 1 inch apart. Press the trimmings together and roll or pat into another ¾-inch thick square. Cut out as many squares as possible, and transfer to the cookie sheet. Dust the tops with a little whole-wheat flour and bake until risen and golden, 10 to 12 minutes.

4 Meanwhile, prepare the sweet date-butter. Put all the ingredients in the bowl of a food processor fitted with a metal blade. Process until smooth, scraping down the sides of the

bowl once or twice. Transfer to a bowl and refrigerate, covered, until ready to serve.

5 Remove sheet to a wire rack and cool, about 2 minutes, then transfer scones to the wire rack to cool until just warm, and serve with sweet-date butter.

Italian Rice Muffins
with honey-amaretto butter

These muffins have *a delicate flavor and texture.*
If possible, use a good arborio rice that has a plump grain,
and *cook it until just al dente* **(firm to the tooth).**

makes 12 muffins

1 cup all-purpose flour
1 Tbsp baking powder
½ tsp baking soda
½ tsp salt
1 egg
¼ cup honey
½ cup milk
2 Tbsp sunflower or vegetable oil
½ tsp almond extract
1 cup cooked rice, lightly packed
2 Amaretti cookies, coarsely crushed

1 Preheat the oven to 400°F. Grease or spray a 12-cup muffin pan or line with paper liners. Sift the flour, baking soda, and salt into a large bowl, and make a generous well in the center.

2 Beat the egg with the honey in another bowl until well blended and foamy. Gradually beat in the milk, oil and almond extract, then whisk in the rice, separating any lumps. Pour into the well and stir lightly until just combined. Do not overmix; the batter should be slightly lumpy.

3 Spoon the batter into the prepared cups, filling each about ⅔ full. Sprinkle the top with a little of the Amaretti crumbs. Bake until risen, golden and springy when pressed, 15 to 20 minutes. Remove pan to a wire rack to cool, about 2 minutes, then remove muffins to the wire rack to cool. Serve with Honey-Amaretto Butter.

honey-amaretto butter
makes about ¼ cup

1 stick unsalted butter, softened
2 Tbsp honey
2 Tbsp Amaretto liqueur

In a small bowl, beat the butter until smooth and creamy, then beat in the honey and Amaretto liqueur until well blended. Spoon onto a piece of wax paper or plastic wrap, and shape into a log about 1 inch thick. Wrap and refrigerate until chilled, about 1 hour. Cut into rounds to serve; allow to soften for a few minutes at room temperature for easier spreading.

Country-apple Scones

These rustic-looking scones are packed with flavor and, because they are *long-lasting and substantial,* make a great fall picnic treat.

makes 8 scones

1⅔ cups all-purpose flour
1½ tsp baking powder
½ tsp baking soda
½ tsp salt
½ tsp ground cinnamon
½ cup sugar
Grated rind of 1 orange
½ stick butter, cut into pieces
2 small dessert apples, peeled, cored, and chopped
½ to ¾ cup buttermilk
½ tsp vanilla extract
2 Tbsp brown sugar
2 Tbsp slivered almonds

1 Preheat the oven to 400°F. Lightly flour a large cookie sheet. Sift the flour, baking powder, baking soda, salt, and cinnamon into a large bowl; stir in the sugar and the grated orange rind.

2 Sprinkle the butter pieces over the flour mixture, and blend in the butter using a pastry blender or your fingertips until the mixture resembles coarse crumbs. Stir in the apples, tossing to coat well with the flour mixture, and make a well in the center.

3 Pour in most of the buttermilk and the vanilla extract, and stir lightly with a fork until a soft dough forms. Add more buttermilk if the dough seems too dry, but do not overmix. Form dough into a rough ball and place on a lightly floured surface; knead 8 to 10 times to blend. Pat the dough into a ¾-inch thick round, about 8 inches in diameter, and transfer to the cookie sheet.

4 Brush the top of the dough with the remaining buttermilk, and sprinkle with the brown sugar and the almonds. Using a sharp knife, score the top deeply into eight wedges. Do not drag the knife through, but maneuver it gently to separate each edge by about ½ inch. Bake until risen and golden, 15 to 20 minutes. Remove to a wire rack to cool to room temperature. Serve warm with raspberry or strawberry preserves.

TIP When making scones or biscuits, avoid over-mixing the fat and flour. Use chilled butter or margarine, and blend these in until the mixture resembles coarse to fine crumbs.

Double Chocolate-chip Muffins

These rich, chocolate muffins make *a great morning snack* with a frothy cappuccino or a glass of cold milk.

makes 10 muffins

1¾ cups all-purpose flour
¼ cup unsweetened cocoa powder
1 Tbsp baking powder
½ tsp salt
½ cup sugar
½ cup semisweet, dark chocolate chips and ¼ cup white chocolate chips
2 eggs
½ cup sunflower or vegetable oil
1 cup milk
1 tsp vanilla extract

1 Preheat the oven to 400°F. Grease or line 10 muffin-pan cups with foil or double-paper liners. Half fill any remaining empty cups in the muffin pan with water to prevent them from scorching. Sift the flour, cocoa powder, baking powder, and salt into a large bowl. Stir in the sugar and chocolate chips, and make a well in the center.

2 In another bowl or 4-cup measure, beat the eggs with the oil until foamy. Gradually beat in the milk and vanilla extract. Pour into the well and stir until just combined. Do not overmix; the batter should be slightly lumpy.

3 Spoon the batter into the prepared cups, filling each about ¾ full. Bake until risen, golden, and springy when pressed with your fingertips, about 20 minutes. Remove pan to a wire rack to cool, about 2 minutes, then remove muffins to the wire rack to cool. Serve warm or at room temperature.

Warm Orange Muffins
with winter dried-fruit salad

These warm, delicate muffins make *a perfect accompaniment to a "winter salad"* of dried fruits. Serve with *fresh whipped cream or sour cream* for a brunch treat.

makes 12 muffins

1¼ cups all-purpose flour
2 tsp baking powder
½ tsp salt
½ cup sugar
½ cup candied orange rind, chopped
1 egg
Grated rind of 1 orange
½ tsp vanilla extract
1 cup buttermilk
½ stick butter or margarine, melted and cooled

1 Preheat the oven to 400°F. Grease or spray a 12-cup muffin pan or line with paper liners. Sift the flour, baking powder, and salt into a large bowl, then stir in the sugar and chopped orange rind, and make a deep well in the center.

2 Beat the egg, orange zest, and vanilla extract in another bowl or 4-cup measure until foamy. Beat in the buttermilk, and melted butter. Pour into the well, and stir lightly until just combined. Do not overmix; the batter should still be slightly lumpy.

3 Spoon the batter into the prepared cups, filling each about three-quarters full. Bake until risen and golden, and a cake tester inserted in the center comes out clean, about 20 minutes. Remove pan to cool on a wire rack for about 2 minutes, then remove the muffins from the pan to cool. Serve warm with the Winter Dried-Fruit Salad.

winter dried-fruit salad

2 cups large, pitted prunes
1½ cups dried, no-soak apricots
1½ cups dried, no-soak pears
¾ cup dried, no-soak peaches
½ cup golden or seedless raisins
1 orange
1 tsp vanilla extract
1 cinnamon stick
2 to 3 cloves
2 to 3 Tbsp sugar or honey, or to taste
Boiling water

Put the prunes, apricots, pears, and peaches in a large bowl, then sprinkle in the raisins. Using a swivel-bladed vegetable peeler, peel the orange rind in long, thin strips, and add to the fruit. Cut the orange in half and squeeze the juice over the fruit, removing any pits. Add the vanilla extract, cinnamon stick, cloves, and the sugar or honey to taste. Pour over enough boiling water to cover the fruit by 1 inch, then cover and allow to stand for at least 1 hour until the fruit is plump and tender. Stir to blend in the flavors (remove the cinnamon stick and cloves if you like), and serve at room temperature or refrigerate to serve chilled.

Biscuits
and
Cookies

Ginger and Coffee Creams

Crisp ginger nut cookies sandwiched together with a coffee cream:
perfect with a large cup of steaming coffee.

makes about 25

1⅔ cups all-purpose flour
2 tsp baking powder
1 tsp bicarbonate of soda
2 tsp ground ginger
1 tsp mixed spice or pumpkin
*   pie spice*
1 Tbsp superfine sugar
7 Tbsp butter or margarine,
*   plus extra for greasing*
⅔ cup light corn syrup

frosting

½ stick butter, softened
¼ cup superfine sugar
1 tsp coffee extract
½ cup confectioners' sugar,
*   sifted*

1 Preheat the oven to 375°F and grease 2 large cookie sheets. Sift all the dry ingredients together into a bowl, stir in the sugar, and make a well in the center. Melt the butter slowly, then stir in the syrup, and pour the mixture into the well. Mix thoroughly to give a soft but not too sticky dough.

2 Scoop up half teaspoons of the mixture and roll into balls. Place on the prepared cookie sheets, leaving some space between the cookies as they will spread during cooking, and flatten them slightly. Bake in the preheated oven for 15 to 20 minutes until set. Leave to cool for a few minutes on the cookie sheets, then remove to a wire rack to cool completely.

3 To prepare the frosting, beat the butter and superfine sugar together with the coffee extract until well blended. Gradually beat in the confectioners' sugar, sifting it into the bowl, and mix to a stiff paste. Sandwich the cookies together with a little frosting; don't be too generous or it will ooze out when you bite into the cookies.

4 Store the cookies for 2 to 3 days in an airtight tin. The frosting will make them go a little soft, but they are very crisp cookies and will not spoil.

Apricot Bars

A delicious apricot purée **is sandwiched between a shortcake mixture to make these** *filling, healthy fruit bars.*

makes 8 bars

1½ cups dried apricots, chopped
4 Tbsp unsweetened orange juice
6 Tbsp polyunsaturated margarine, melted
4 Tbsp honey
½ cup semolina flour
1 cup plus 2 Tbsp all-purpose flour

1 Lightly grease a 7-inch square cake pan. Place the apricots in a pan with the orange juice and simmer for 5 minutes. Drain if the juice has not been absorbed by the fruit.

2 Heat the margarine and honey in a pan until melted. Add the semolina and flour and mix well. Press half of this mixture into the base of the prepared cake pan. Spoon on the fruit mixture and top with the remaining semolina mix, covering the fruit completely.

3 Bake in the oven at 375°F for 35 minutes until golden. Cool for 5 minutes in the pan, then cut into eight bars. Remove from the pan and leave to cool completely.

Almond Tile Cookies

These popular French cookies **are so called because they resemble** *the curved roof tiles seen all over France.*

makes about 30 cookies

½ cup whole blanched almonds, lightly toasted
½ cup superfine sugar
3 Tbsp unsalted butter, softened
2 egg whites
½ tsp almond extract
¼ cup all-purpose flour, sifted
¾ cup flaked almonds

1 Process the toasted almonds with 2 tablespoons of the sugar until fine crumbs form. Pour into a small bowl; set aside.

2 Preheat the oven to 400°F. Generously grease two cookie sheets. In a medium bowl with an electric mixer, beat the butter until creamy, about 30 seconds. Add the remaining sugar, and beat until light and fluffy, about 1 minute. Gradually beat in the egg whites and almond extract until well-blended. Sift over the flour and fold into the butter mixture, then fold in the reserved almond-sugar mixture.

3 Begin by working in batches of four cookies on each sheet. Drop tablespoonfuls of batter about 6 inches apart on a greased cookie sheet. With the back of a moistened spoon, spread each mound of batter into very thin 3-inch rounds. Each round should be transparent. If you make a few holes, the batter will spread and fill them in. Sprinkle the tops with some flaked almonds.

4 Bake, one sheet at a time, until the edges are browned and the centers just golden, about 4 to 5 minutes. Remove from the cookie sheet to a wire rack and, working quickly, use a thin-bladed metal palette knife to loosen the edge of a hot cookie and transfer to a rolling pin. Gently press down the sides to shape each cookie over it.

5 If the cookies become too firm to transfer, return the cookie sheet to the oven for 30 seconds to soften, then proceed as above. When cool, transfer immediately to airtight containers in single layers.

Lemon Madeleines

Madeleines are a French cookie-cake *baked in pretty shell-shaped molds*. **They are delicious for breakfast or anytime.**

makes about 12 cookies

2 eggs
¾ cup confectioners' sugar
Grated rind of 1 large lemon
1 Tbsp lemon juice
1 tsp baking powder
*1 cup plus 1 Tbsp all-purpose
    flour, sifted*
*¾ stick unsalted butter, melted
    and cooled*
*Confectioners' sugar, for
    dusting*

1 Preheat the oven to 375°F. Lightly grease a 12-cup madeleine mold. In a large bowl with an electric mixer, beat the eggs and sugar until light and pale, and a slowly falling ribbon forms when the beaters are lifted from the bowl, 5 to 7 minutes. Gently fold in the lemon rind and juice.

2 Add the baking powder to the flour and, beginning and ending with flour, alternately fold in the flour and butter in four or five batches. Allow the batter to rest for 10 minutes. Spoon the batter into prepared molds.

3 Bake until a toothpick inserted into the center of a madeleine comes out clean, 12 to 15 minutes, rotating the mold from front to back three-quarters through cooking time. Remove from the oven and turn the madeleines out onto a wire rack immediately. Allow to cool completely. Store in airtight containers and dust with confectioners' sugar before serving.

Chocolate Madeleines

This version of the *classic madeleine* is made with cocoa powder *for a rich chocolate flavor.*

makes about 36 cookies

4 Tbsp unsweetened cocoa powder (preferably Dutch-processed)
3 Tbsp hot water
3 eggs
1 cup superfine sugar
2 tsp vanilla extract
1¼ cups cake flour
¾ tsp baking powder
¼ tsp salt
1½ sticks unsalted butter, softened
Confectioners' sugar, for dusting

TIP Madeleines are best eaten within a day or two of baking as they tend to dry out on storage.

1 Preheat the oven to 350°F. Lightly grease a 12-cup madeleine mold. In a small bowl, dissolve the cocoa powder in hot water until completely smooth. Set aside to cool, then beat in the eggs, sugar, and vanilla extract. Continue beating until the mixture is light and creamy, about 2 to 3 minutes.

2 Into a bowl, sift together the flour, baking powder, and salt. Add half the chocolate-egg mixture and butter, and beat with an electric mixer on a low speed until well blended. Increase the speed to medium and beat for 1 minute more until smooth and light. Gently fold in the remaining chocolate-egg mixture in 2 batches.

3 Using a small ladle or large spoon, fill the madeleine cup molds almost full. Bake until a toothpick inserted in the center of the madeleine comes out clean, about 10 to 12 minutes. Rotate the molds from the front to the back halfway through cooking.

4 Remove the molds to a wire rack and unmold the madeleines onto the rack immediately. Cool the molds and repeat with the remaining batter. Store in airtight containers and dust with confectioners' sugar before serving.

Apple Drop Biscuits

This healthy variation of a breakfast favorite is *filled with chunks of crisp apple* **which are complemented by the** *cinnamon spiced yogurt sauce.*

makes 4 servings

For the biscuits

½ cup whole-wheat flour
1 tsp baking powder
1 tsp superfine sugar
1 medium egg, beaten
⅓ cup skim milk
1 green dessert apple, cored
    and chopped

For the yogurt sauce

⅔ cup low-fat plain yogurt
½ tsp ground cinnamon
1 tsp honey

1 Sift the flour and baking powder for the biscuits into a mixing bowl and stir in the sugar. Make a well in the center and beat in the egg and milk to make a smooth batter. Stir in the apple and raisins, mixing well.

2 Brush a heavy-based, non-stick skillet with a little oil and warm over a medium heat. Divide the batter into eight equal portions and drop four portions into the skillet, spacing them well apart. Cook gently for 2 to 3 minutes until the top of each drop biscuit begins to bubble. Turn the biscuits over and cook for 1 minute.

3 Transfer to a warmed plate and keep hot while cooking the remaining biscuits. Mix the yogurt sauce ingredients together in a bowl and serve with the hot drop biscuits.

Coffee and Chocolate Chip Shortbreads

For the best flavor, *always make shortbread with butter.* **These shortbreads** *can be stored in an airtight tin* **for up to two weeks.**

makes about 20 biscuits

1½ sticks butter, plus extra for
    greasing
1¼ cups all-purpose flour
2 tsp freeze-dried instant
    coffee granules
½ cup confectioners' sugar,
    sifted
Few drops of vanilla extract
⅓ cup fine chocolate chips

1 Cream the butter in a bowl until soft, then gradually work in all the remaining ingredients except the chocolate. Continue working the dough until it begins to come together, then add the chocolate and knead into a firm dough. Shape into a roll about 15 inches long, then cover in plastic wrap and chill in the refrigerator for about 1 hour.

2 Preheat the oven to 350°F and lightly grease two cookie sheets. Slice the dough into 24 pieces, then place on the cookie sheets and flatten slightly with a fork. Bake the shortbreads in the preheated oven for 20 to 25 minutes until lightly golden.

3 Allow the shortbreads to cool for 1 to 2 minutes on the cookie sheets, then transfer them carefully with a palette knife to a wire rack until completely cold.

Index